my visit to the
DINOSAURS

HORNED DINOSAUR
STYRASCO SAURUS

my visit to the
DINOSAURS

by ALIKI

A Harper Trophy Book

Thomas Y. Crowell Company   New York

LET'S-READ-AND-FIND-OUT BOOKS

Let's-Read-and-Find-Out Books are edited by Dr. Roma Gans, Professor Emeritus of Childhood Education, Teachers College, Columbia University, and Dr. Franklyn M. Branley, Astronomer Emeritus and former Chairman of the American Museum–Hayden Planetarium. Text and illustrations for each of the more than 100 books in the series are checked for accuracy by an expert in the relevant field. Other titles available in paperback are listed below. Look for them at your local bookstore or library.

My Visit to the Dinosaurs
Copyright © 1969 by Aliki Brandenberg
All rights reserved. No part of this book may be used or
reproduced in any manner whatsoever without written permission
except in the case of brief quotations embodied in critical
articles and reviews. Printed in the United States of America.
For information address Harper & Row, Publishers, Inc.,
10 East 53rd Street, New York, N.Y. 10022. Published simultaneously
in Canada by Fitzhenry & Whiteside Limited, Toronto.
Library of Congress Catalog Card Number: 70-78255
ISBN 0-690-57403-7
ISBN 0-06-445006-6 (pbk.)

my visit to the
DINOSAURS

Yesterday I went to see the dinosaurs.
I went with my father and my little sister.
The man showed us where to find the dinosaurs.
He took us up in a big elevator.

VISIT THE
DINOSAURS

UP
DOWN

1

We walked down a hall, turned a corner—and there
    they were. Skeletons.
Real dinosaur skeletons.
They were standing in a room bigger than a house.
One skeleton was almost as long as the room.
It looked scary.

My father told my sister and me not to be afraid.
Dinosaurs lived millions of years ago.
No dinosaurs are alive today.

FIRST DINOSAUR HALL

EARLY DINOSAUR HALL

FIRE HOSE INSIDE

QUIET

3

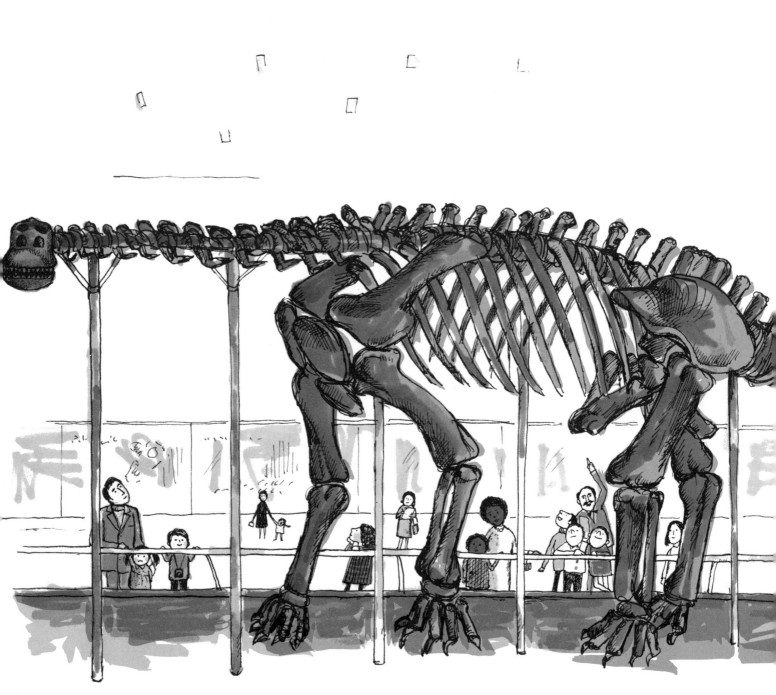

I took a picture of the long dinosaur,
    BRONTOSAURUS.
Then I went over and looked closer.

The skeleton was wired together. Heavy rods held
    it up.
I could see that some of the bones were not real.
They were made of plaster.
What a job it must have been to put this huge
    puzzle together.
How could anyone know where all the pieces fit?

When the dinosaurs died, they were covered with sand and mud. They were buried for millions of years.

The sand and mud turned into rocks, and the dinosaurs' bones became fossils.

In 1822 the first dinosaur fossil was found.
It was found by accident.

After that, many diggers went looking for fossils.
They dug in the rocky earth.

They found fossil bones of dinosaurs.

Some diggers found fossil eggs, which the dinosaurs
had laid in sandy pits.

They even found fossil baby dinosaurs.

It is hard work to take fossils from the ground.
They are often embedded in solid rock.

Paleontologists studied the fossils carefully.

A paleontologist is a scientist who studies animals
and plants of the past.

Paleontologists know when dinosaurs lived and how
dinosaurs lived.

They know what dinosaurs ate.

GORGOSAURUS
MEAT EATER

Some dinosaurs ate meat, and some ate plants.
Giant dinosaurs and duckbill dinosaurs ate plants.
So did horned dinosaurs and armored dinosaurs
and plated dinosaurs.
Many of the plant eaters spent most of their lives
in the water.

CORYTHOSAURUS
(DUCK BILL DINOSAUR)
PLANT EATER

STYRACOSAURUS
(HORNED DINOSAUR)
PLANT EATER

ANKYLOSAURUS
(ARMORED DINOSAUR)
PLANT EATER

BRONTOSAURUS was a plant eater.

This is the way it looked when it was alive.

Brontosaurus reached down with its long neck in the swamps and ate water plants.

It could lie low and hide from an enemy.

Its eyes were high on its flat head.

It could peek out without being seen.

BRACHIOSAURUS was another giant dinosaur that lived in the water and ate plants.
It was the biggest and heaviest dinosaur there ever was.

15

Another plant eater was TRACHODON, a duckbill.
It had feet that were webbed, like a duck's.
It was a good swimmer.

Trachodon had jaws shaped like a duck's bill.
The jaws were full of teeth.
Trachodon had 1,600 flat teeth to crush and grind
  its food.

PROTOCERATOPS was a horned dinosaur.

ANKYLOSAURUS was an armored dinosaur.

These dinosaurs ate plants, too, but they lived on
   land.
They looked so unappetizing that meat-eating dinosaurs left them alone.
Who would want to bite their thick, leathery skin,
   covered with bony spikes and plates?

Meat-eating dinosaurs were fast, fierce hunters.

A hungry meat eater like ALLOSAURUS ate any animal it could find.

It was not even afraid to attack Brontosaurus, which was twice its size.

Allosaurus ran on two strong legs.

It caught its prey in its short arms and ripped it apart with big, pointed claws.

Allosaurus ate its food with long, sharp teeth.

21

My father, my sister, and I went to another hall
   and looked at more skeletons.
There were so many to see that we had to hurry.

HORNED DINOSAUR

23

DIPLODOCUS was the longest dinosaur. Its body was so big, and its head and mouth so small, that it had to eat its plant food almost without stopping, in order to satisfy its hunger.

ORNITHOLESTES was a small, swift dinosaur.
Some of the animals it ate were birds.

OVIRAPTOR was another little dinosaur.
It had no teeth at all.
It ate the eggs of other dinosaurs.

25

We saw a plated dinosaur, fierce-looking
STEGOSAURUS.

It had big, bony plates covering its back, and a
spiked tail to swing at its enemies.

We saw horned dinosaurs, too.
MONOCLONIUS had only one horn.

STYRACOSAURUS had a horn on its nose and a
frill of spikes around its neck.

And TRICERATOPS had three horns on its head—
one on its nose and one over each eye.
A big, fan-shaped bone protected its neck.
My father said Triceratops could defend itself even
against TYRANNOSAURUS REX.
I wondered who Tyrannosaurus Rex was.

Then I saw it.

TYRANNOSAURUS REX was king of all the dinosaurs. And the fiercest.

When it walked the earth on its huge hind legs, Tyrannosaurus towered over all the other dinosaurs.

It grabbed them with its small forearms.

It tore them apart with pointed claws and ate them with its long, sharp teeth.

I had to stand far away from Tyrannosaurus to take its picture.

My father and my sister looked tiny next to it.

I was glad Tyrannosaurus Rex wasn't alive any more.

When you go to the museum, you will see what I mean.

TYRANNOSAURUS

33

ABOUT THE AUTHOR-ILLUSTRATOR

Aliki worked in many phases of the art field before she began illustrating and writing children's books. Now, when she is not too busy with books, she likes making dolls, puppets, and scenery for the family puppet theater.

Aliki Brandenberg grew up in Philadelphia and graduated from the Museum College of Art. She and her husband, Franz Brandenberg, lived in Switzerland for several years and traveled to many countries.

Now Mr. and Mrs. Brandenberg live in New York City. Their travels take them to many museums with their two young children, Jason and Alexa. It is, in fact, these trips that acquainted the Brandenbergs with the dinosaurs.